# a long exposure of undoing

sarah "sam" saltiel

A STORM OF BLUE BOOK

Copyright © 2019 Sarah "Sam" Saltiel

All rights reserved. No part of this publication may be reproduced, distributed, or transmitted in any form or by any means, including photocopying, recording, or other electronic or mechanical methods, without the prior written permission of the publisher, except in the case of brief quotations embodied in critical reviews and certain other noncommercial uses permitted by copyright law.

ISBN: 978-0-578-59819-2

Library of Congress Control Number: 2019916814

I have tried to recreate events, locales and conversations from my memories of them. In order to maintain their anonymity in some instances I have changed the names of individuals and places. I may have changed some identifying characteristics and details such as physical properties, occupations, and places of residence.

Front cover by Zoë Blair-Schlagenhauf.
Printed by IngramSpark.

First printing edition 2020.

Distributed by Storm of Blue Press.

**Foreword**

In the beginning of 2019, I was working on The Cassandra Transcripts, a project that entailed interviewing people about their experiences with gender and mental illness. I felt and feel that it is one of the most important projects I have ever worked on, but the difficult content of the work aggravated my mental illness to a dangerous degree. While in the midst of my depressive period, I was sexually assaulted. This poetry chapbook is about the experience of intimacy through the lens of trauma and dissociation, but it's also about investing hope in your own resilience. While it's likely that there will be a "next depressive episode", there can also be a "next time you laugh" or "next time something makes you feel just a little bit lighter". Though much of the writing is bleak, the fact that I'm still around to write it is testament to that.

With that in mind, I owe so much to my friends around me: the ones that read through multiple iterations of this chapbook, and the ones that sat with me and held my hand this winter, even when I didn't have the energy to talk. Each one of you gives me a reason to smile.

Sarah "Sam" Saltiel

a long exposure of undoing


my mother texted me the winter before i left chicago
to say that she had a dream that i moved out to the desert and was happy

       she told me that this was a good omen for my next year—

              every time she imagines me, (she imagines me) somewhere warm


on my way back home, my foot slipped on the ice,
blood clots
      turned to glue between my skin and my clothes.


      that january
the temperature dropped to below -20 — i invited a girl to stay over —
i found out she was too good for me, that i felt nothing    ?

the second night, after everyone went to bed, drunk in the way that you can only get drunk
in the dead of winter, i sat on the couch alone, spinning. i (imagined me)
walking out into the cold in my tank top and the flannel pajamas my grandmother gave me
for christmas, feet dragging through the snow until my footprints got longer and
coldstopped. i have learned to sit with these thoughts and leave them untouched—

\*\*\*

i submitted a piece to a magazine about being in class with someone who sexually assaulted me.

                                                Not emotionally raw enough

                    was the feedback. when they asked if i wanted
                    to change it, i told them no.


i didn't know how to appease someone who wanted me




                                            gutted

\*\*\*

shortly,

i fell in love with someone                              —you—

        in love with someone else. you were the opposite of a ghost

i got you, corporeal, but your wound was elsewhere.

when you kissed me i cried

***

                                those months, my body hollowed my bed with hours of
transcribing interviews, posting them online, records of
sadness. i spent more time listening to recordings of
people's voices than i did talking to actual people.

i slept with two people that winter — i tried (?)

        to thaw?— i     tried

the first one was much older than me. i texted his address to a friend as the mist walked me to his
door. halfway through sex he called me young, guttural groaning     so
i unfroze from his sheets and left before either of us came— i

                                                                                   tried?

a few weeks after i slept with him, he messaged me about the interviews,
asking to meet up. to *talk.*
i told him if he was so interested in my
                                    *thoughts,*
                                    he should read the transcript about my life.

                  (did

                                      he

                                                          try?)

the next day i received a message saying he was sorry if he had hurt me, that he didn't know what i
had gone through. i didn't know what wrong he thought he had done me, or how he thought it was
more wrong if i came from a place swallowed by sadness.
                i left the message unopened for days.
i didn't want to assuage his guilt. i just wanted                       (?)
                                        to sleep.

                    while i transcribed, i had conversations with their echoes, and when my
          voice appeared on the
recordings, i had conversations with my own, sometimes repeating the same words i had
said months before, not remembering that i had said them. i echo i am echo caught

               ?it

                                         ?


it was the sort of thing that made me want to go
        in the middle of the night
for a run all the way out to lake michigan,
pull my shoes off,
and steep myself in the water that has been here since before the



                great chicago fire.
the lake will be here far longer than me.

\*\*\*

in the desert my lips crack

i swallow sand, unwound

the second person i slept with shared my ex's name, one letter shifted
i wondered if i was rewinding my chicago self— how can i undo four years of shell shivering?

when i held him he said that it was lucky he didn't have emotions.
he didn't explain when i asked but

i thought i knew

***

in the same vein          ?i performed an art piece called, the moment you realize your suicidal ideation is back after being gone for months. i walked cold-hollowed around a mattress in my scooby doo pajama shirt and cookie monster shorts          folding laundry.

i said the piece was about coping with head-heaviness of death and still having to get up and do things like
laundry and                    love
and sex
and taking out the trash.

when i was done the professor looked and said,

So what? You're sad? That's not art.

\*\*\*

Q. What's your name?

a. oh. this one is tough. can i skip this? i'm sorry. words are hard today.

Q. How long have you been sad?

a. long enough that it's stopped being beautiful. i am just tired.

Q. Where does your sadness come from?
a. too freudian to say my parents. if i say assault or abuse, it's true but not all the truth. i think i am just sad. i think i was sad long before any of this.

Q. Will you always be sad?

a. hope not. i'm moving to the desert.

Q. Is there anything you want?

a. to touch someone.

Q. Why don't you?

a. can't.

Q. Why not?

a. just sad.

\*\*\*

at my father's house during spring break, i sat working. he yelled at me for having my bag out on the table in the process of my using it.
it felt like a shorthand— my active use of an object left too many traces of me behind—

i...                           ectoplasm

every morning, when i walked into the kitchen, his wife jumped, as if she had seen a ghost.

\*\*\*

later, in new orleans, i hurricaned on bourbon street,

beside a man i barely knew, i listened to when the saints come marching in.

he turned to me, light,   bright   eyes

           glittering

                    said, I went to a jazz festival where there were cutting edge musicians. And this... a high school band could do this. A good high school band... but a high school band could do this. But both experiences are meaningful and I don't quite understand why.

that night, i almost watched the saints disappear  
didn't tell any of the people with me how much it meant to me  
                            i almost? disappear?

\*\*\*

The things I did the two days after I was assaulted: I got up. I taught dance. I made myself food –two sausages and a mango. I returned to my bed and slept for five hours, not enough. I took a bath and floated for a while, touching my body. I bought dishwashing soap and coffee. I talked with my roommates. I did research for a trip. I washed the dishes and cried. I called my friend and sat with her on the phone. I lay in my bed drawing until I couldn't. cancelled dance. didn't do my lab report. drank three cups of tea. walked in a circle around five blocks. went to dinner, when my friend's father sat next to me,

                                                              my muscles
                                                                   snapped

                                                                                             tight—
                                                                                            i— ?

\*\*\*

And I since I was feeling really sad and craving company and physical contact, I actively made the worst choice that I could have

And we ended up texting afterwards

And he said something to the effect of, "what if I come over and cuddle"

And I was like, "sure but I'm not having sex with you"

I was mostly just too tired to kick him out

It's as if he thought he could wear me down by the sheer number of times that he tried

I really don't know what I expected

Because that seems like the only possible outcome from that situation

He was never going to respect the boundary that I set

the day i filed a title ix report you sat with me and i said (or thought?) that i didn't know how to keep living in a place where i have so much anger

i want you in the long term, i short term myself, undo my want

\*\*\*

*SCOOBY DOO interviews 50 people about their sadness. spends hours transcribing those interviews, finds phantoms between the words.*

*SCOOBY DOO: let's see who the ghost was the whole time*

*SCOOBY DOO pulls off the                           mask?*

                                        *SCOOBY DOO deserts*

\*\*\*

i was cold?

because i wanted an excuse to touch you

when you kissed me i cried	there will be a point

when i will stop loving you / loving love for love's sake — is that when the healing will no longer be worth the pain?

                      i cannot tell

if this is a scab that i keep picking at until infection layers sleeping into my skin, or if this is a bone that i'm breaking again so that it can set right this time.

i want to have enough sex with you that it becomes boring ritual and our legs cramp and our jaws lock up —	unfinished, shocked —	i left in the morning
                                  after you kissed me

i leave, am still leaving, lungs misted, i unfinish(?)
i want to cling like the brown, wet leaves stuck to the sidewalk – they will destroy (themselves), leaving layers to wade through
i residue	you

\*\*\*

you noun me. i verb.

                        next year i will move to the desert
                        next year will you visit me
                        next year will you love me

                                      we undid(?)

                                                  you'll find me folding laundry

"Sarah "Sam" Saltiel is a queer nonbinary artist and writer currently based in Albuquerque, New Mexico. Her work generally deals with what it means to be a body in space, particularly as it relates to gender or mental illness. In 2012 she was diagnosed with Major Depressive Disorder and Generalized Anxiety Disorder and has since sought to create pieces that enter into the conversation about neurodiverse narratives.

One such piece is The Cassandra Transcripts, started in fall of 2018. It is an ongoing (as of the publication of this chapbook) series of interviews about the intersections between femininity and mental illness. Saltiel collaborated with over 50 people to produce transcripts and portraits about what it means to navigate and grapple with those identities. She has since started The Hercules Transcripts, a counterpart about the intersections between masculinity and mental illness. More information about both projects and the rest of Saltiel's work can be found on her website at sarahsamsaltiel.com.

Additional LGBTQ projects, literary collections, and intentional vulnerability can be found at stormofblue.com.

If you or a loved one is dealing with mental illness or trauma, the list below entails a few of the mental health
resources that are available:

Samaritans: 877-870-4673
Mental Health Resources: socialworklicensemap.com
The Suicide Prevention Hotline: 1-800-273-8255
The Trevor Project: thetrevorproject.org
Students Against Depression: studentsagainstdepression.org
Recovery Warriors: recoverywarriors.com
National Sexual Assault Hotline: 800-656-4673

www.ingramcontent.com/pod-product-compliance
Lightning Source LLC
Chambersburg PA
CBHW051151290426
44108CB00019B/2681